Theme from

Ladies
in Lavender

by Nigel Hess

Arranged for violin with piano accompaniment

FABER *ff* MUSIC

Theme from

Ladies in Lavender

NIGEL HESS

This edition © 2009 by Faber Music Ltd
Bloomsbury House
74–77 Great Russell Street
London WC1B 3DA
Cover design by Lydia Merrills-Ashcroft
Printed in England by Caligraving Ltd
All rights reserved

ISBN10: 0-571-53396-5
EAN13: 978-0-571-53396-1

To buy Faber Music publications or to find out about the full range of titles available
please contact your local music retailer or Faber Music sales enquiries:

Faber Music Ltd, Burnt Mill, Elizabeth Way, Harlow CM20 2HX
Tel: +44 (0) 1279 82 89 82   Fax: +44 (0) 1279 82 89 83
sales@fabermusic.com   fabermusic.com

VIOLIN MUSIC FROM FABER MUSIC

Fingerprints for Violin

EDITED BY MARY COHEN

A great collection of original, new music for players of Grade 1–4 standard. Each composer has tried to capture the essence of what makes them who they are and have left a musical 'fingerprint' for you to discover.

ISBN 0-571-52258-0

Real Repertoire for Violin

EDITED BY MARY COHEN

Essential repertoire for the intermediate violinist: a lasting inspiration to players everywhere.

ISBN 0-571-52155-X

Technique Takes Off!

MARY COHEN

Original, imaginative studies for solo violin covering a wide range of left and right-hand skills.

ISBN 0-571-51307-7

More Technique Takes Off!

MARY COHEN

Unaccompanied duets and studies, providing an imaginative and exciting course in developing vibrato, double-stopping and shifting.

ISBN 0-571-52484-2

To buy Faber Music publications or to find out about the full range of titles available please contact your local music retailer or Faber Music sales enquiries:

Faber Music Ltd, Burnt Mill, Elizabeth Way, Harlow CM20 2HX
Tel: +44 (0) 1279 82 89 82   Fax: +44 (0) 1279 82 89 83
sales@fabermusic.com   fabermusic.com   expressprintmusic.com